A GUIDE TO HANUKKAH
AND PURIM

A GUIDE TO
HANUKKAH
AND
PURIM

by

RABBI S. M. LEHRMAN, M.A., Ph.D.
Tyrwhitt Scholar, Cambridge

JEWISH CHRONICLE PUBLICATIONS
London

Published by
JEWISH CHRONICLE PUBLICATIONS
37 *Furnival Street, London, EC4*
© S. M. Lehrman, 1958

Second Impression, 1962

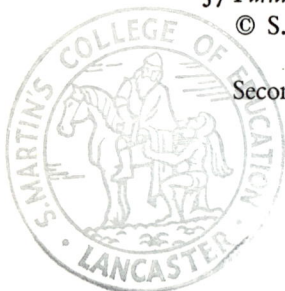

Dedicated in lasting friendship to
ISAAC PRESMAN

Made and printed in Great Britain by
THE SHARON PRESS
31 *Furnival Street, London, EC4*

CONTENTS

PART I HANUKKAH

v

PART II PURIM

PART I

HANUKKAH

CHAPTER I

JEW MEETS GREEK

IN THE thirty-one chapters which comprise the two Books of the Maccabees in the Apocrypha, the story which is Hanukkah is graphically told. The reader should turn to these sources and learn, at first-hand, the causes of this duel between Jew and Syrian-Greek, the tale of the ensuing pitched struggles, and their triumphant sequel.

The essence of the story is told in the twenty-four Hebrew words which form the fifth stanza of the *Ma'oz Tsur*. Their English translation is not so laconic of expression. 'The Grecians gathered themselves together against me in the days of the Hasmoneans. They broke down the walls of my towers and defiled all the oils. But from the last of the remaining flasks, a miracle was wrought for the beloved, and men of understanding appointed eight days for song and praise.'

The Cause of the Strife

The actual struggle, of which Hanukkah is the glorious climax, began in 175 B.C.E., when Antiochus Epiphanes (the Revealed), whom men called Epimanes (Madman), on account of his cruelty and arrogance, became King of Syria. But in reality, the clash between the two cultures which Hebraism and Hellenism represented started much earlier. It began when Jew perhaps first met Greek in the wake of the global conquests of Alexander the Great (356-323 B.C.E.). It was this peerless conqueror who, in the short space of eight years, overran the entire eastern half of the then-known world, stopping only on the banks of the River Indus, because his soldiers refused to follow him into the unknown beyond.

Alexander brought the Jews into the orbit of Hellenism, an impact which was to register a deep impression on the development of Judaism, as on the culture of humanity generally. In *Midrashic* literature and popular legend, Alexander figures as a knight-errant in shining armour invested with an aureole of shrewd wisdom. Under his rule, the Jews enjoyed independence politically, and autonomy spiritually; but when Antiochus came to power the pendulum swung violently the other way. The spark was kindled when the semi-demented Emperor decided to prohibit the Jews, under the penalty of death, from observing their ancestral faith. Instead, they were to worship the gods of the Greeks, prominent among whom was Zeus, whose huge statue had been placed in the Temple at Jerusalem.

Incensed at this sacrilege, the Jews, under the heroic leadership of the Hasmoneans, whom we shall describe in due course, resolved to make a bold bid for freedom. Death for an ideal was preferable to a life of shame, wickedness and lust.

A word of explanation is necessary at this point. Though the Greeks in the golden period, which was Hellas, had made a tremendous impact in the realm of architecture and sculpture, poetry and philosophy, oratory and drama, yet behind this brilliant façade lurked vice and cruelty. The gods whom they worshipped, and on whom they modelled their own personal lives, did not stand for justice and purity of living. Sad to relate, it was this baser side of Greek civilization which was adopted by the Macedonians, and later by the Syrians.

Traitors from Within

The aim of Antiochus—to disrupt an alien, stubborn faith within his dominion—was helped by the dissensions which existed in Israel's ranks. There were some Jews who were blinded by the spurious after-glow of former Greek culture, preferring to be known as Hellenist Jews. When the royal edict proclaimed that all subjects of the king should be one people, conforming to one set of laws, temporal and spiritual, they lost their nerve. They followed Greek fashions, adopted their language, changed their Hebrew names to Hellenic parallels, and frequented Greek arenas and gymnasia. This pursuit of Hellenism was so feverish that it infected the High Priests at the time, mostly underlings of conquerors whom they had bribed for the favour of their office. When assimilation was at its height, the struggle began.

Before we come to contrast the two opposing cultural and ideological forces of Hellenism and Hebraism, two things must be made absolutely clear. First: it was not antisemitism which prompted Antiochus to issue these harsh decrees, but a determined effort to fuse his subjected nations into one huge family, of which he was the royal father. Second: the Maccabean struggle was unique, in that it was not fought for the extension of Judea's borders, or for the personal aggrandizement of its rulers. Is not the lesson of Hanukkah that which is proclaimed by Zechariah (iv: 6): *'This is the word of the Lord unto Zerubabel, saying: "Not by might, nor by power, but by My spirit, saith the Lord of hosts?"'* And is it not significant that in the account found in the Talmud of the struggle (*Shabbat* 21b), the military achievement is passed over in complete silence? It only recounts the story of the cruse of oil, undefiled by the enemy and bearing the unbroken seal of the High Priest, with sufficient oil for only one day's kindling, but which enabled the Perpetual Lamp to burn on brightly for eight days when a fresh supply of levitically-pure oil was obtained.

It was against this spirit of idealism and martyrdom which invested the noble band of the faithful, that the mighty, disciplined forces of the enemy lashed their onslaughts of fury in vain. The handful of Maccabeans, whom the call of conscience had inflamed with desperate courage, fought with weapons in their hands and faith in their hearts. Their triumph still rings out across the ages, making the name Maccabean synonymous with heroism for a religious ideal. Others before the Hasmoneans had displayed courage and self-sacrifice on the battlefield, but such manifestations were rarely motivated by instincts other than self-preservation, or by a desire for gain. This was the first time in history that a battle was fought purely for the survival of a faith first promulgated at Sinai, thousands of years ago.

CHAPTER 2

HELLENISM VERSUS HEBRAISM

THE customs in the synagogue and the home are intended to emphasize the antipodic views on life held by Jew and Greek when they met face to face on the ancient battlefields of Modin and Beth-Horon, Beth-Zur and Beth-Zechariah, Acra and Eleasa—where Judah the Maccabean, perhaps the bravest of the five sons of Mattathias—fought his last battle. The lights that are kindled at sunset on each eve of the festival, are symbolic of the hope that the faith of the Jew will one day banish the darkness of hate which still hangs like a pall over much of the earth's surface. The flames of the Menorah are intended to evoke anew the enthusiasm which blazed so brightly in the hearts of those heroes of old.

Everything about Hanukkah proclaims the undying faith characteristic of the loyal Jew. Yet it would be wrong to believe that Judaism fosters an easy optimism. Like Prometheus in Greek mythology, the Jew it was who first brought down from heaven the everlasting fire, in an attempt to illumine with it the dark places of the earth. Like Prometheus, too, he has been chained to the rock of suffering as a 'reward' of his efforts. That the Jew has not faltered in his mission as torchbearer of justice, is to a large extent due to the message of

Hanukkah which exhorted him to kindle anew, at the altar of Judaism, the torches of faith and hope.

Athens and Jerusalem

The geographical distance between these two cities which, together with Rome, were the three main cradles of civilization, pales into insignificance when paralleled with their spiritual and ideological poles which stood so far asunder as to belong to two alien worlds. The view of life sponsored by Athens was inimical to that preached from Zion's academies. When Jew met Greek for the first time in the open, it was not the ordinary meeting of two peoples, or even of two kinds of civilization. It was a clash between two philosophies of life, abruptly opposed to, and mutually exclusive of, each other. It was, to all effects, a duel between the Eternal Creator of the universe, that invisible Omnipotent, Omnipresent and Omniscient Being who had in a miraculous way *revealed* ethical and positive ideals to the whole of mankind, and Zeus, the deity who had made Olympus his residence, whose delight was in nature, in the partaking of nectar and ambrosia, and whose pursuits and pre-occupations were far from godly.

Impassable barriers separated Jew and Greek also in the fields of religion and morality. The Hellenist deified Nature herself, making the material world around him the object of his worship. The Jew deified the Creator of Nature, paying obeisance to the Spirit of God which hovered over the surface of the globe. Whereas the Hellenist stressed the human in the divine, the Jew stressed the divine in the human. Each pilgrim on earth was coined in the image of God; each being, to employ the Rabbinic phrase, 'a partner in the work of Creation.' What respect, for instance, could the Jew, indoctrined as he constantly was with the highest ideals for the good life, have for these 'gods' of Olympus, portrayed even by those who worshipped them, as subjected to the whims and passions of ordinary mortals?

While the Hellenist paid homage, first and foremost, to external beauty and physical prowess, the Jew praised inner loveliness and heroism born of idealism. In Athens, life was a cult of *beauty*; in Jerusalem, it was an insistence on *duty*. Greece, in its halcyon days, was a paradise of pleasure and beauty, crowned by magnificent temples, spacious buildings and colossal amphitheatres, such as are being constantly revealed by the curious spade of the excavator. Despite this glamorous façade, the loyal Jew preferred martyrdom to a betrayal of his ancestral teachings. It was against this forced betrayal, that the Hasmoneans fought in the face of overwhelming odds—and triumphed. Echoes of this victory are heard in the martial tune to which the words of the *Ma'oz Tsur* have been wedded, in the benedictions pronounced over the festive lights, and in the Hallel recited on each of the eight days of Hanukkah.

An Eternal Duel

Thus understood, Hanukkah is not merely a cele-bration of a victory which took place in ancient Judea in the years 167-165 B.C.E., but a recurring factor throughout Jewish history. That is why our festival has fired the imagination of the Jew in all times, till it has now become one of the shining gems in the crown of Jewish festivals and to which, incidentally, the Jewish State has given a new lease of life. For in the Galut, its observance had become formal, stereotyped, mechanical, consisting of a few supplementary items to the synagogue service, and of a few home customs. Yet without the meticulous observance of these outward formalities, who knows whether the miracle which is now the Jewish State, and the Maccabean spirit by which it was established and now being run, would have been possible? Little wonder that from the beginnings of the national movement, our festival was always cherished with love and respect. Herzl tells us in a memorable passage in one of his Essays (Quoted in Hertz's *Book of Jewish Thoughts*), that it was the light of the Hanukkah Menorah which first kindled within him thoughts of belonging to the Jewish people.

Hanukkah can only be observed in the spirit of its Hasmonean founders, if the Jew refuses to identify the moral with the pleasant, or to regard his stay on earth as a round of physical delights. To him, cradled in the spirit of the Torah, 'the beauty of holiness' will always be the *leitmotif* of his life's symphony. To honour the memory of the Maccabeans means to renounce impurity of thought and licentiousness of action, and to set up in their stead the control of unworthy passions, with a resolve to improve the soul and discipline desires. *To the Hellenist, everything that was externally beautiful was good; to the Jew, everything that was inwardly good was beautiful.*

Jew and Greek differed both in their *insight* into, as well as in their *outlook* on, life. The dichotomy was also marked in the brusque opposition of their characters. The political tyranny of the Greek oppressors was matched by their dissolute life, which had infected philosophers in the academy, no less than the man in the street. Wherever the Jew turned, his feelings of decency and morality were outraged.

When religious persecution was added to these outrages, the patience of the loyal bands of Jews was exhausted. The match was now applied to the dangerous barrels of gunpowder the Syrian-Greeks had heaped up since Antiochus Epiphanes mounted the throne— a throne once occupied by the famous son of Philip of Macedon, whose aim was to win over stubbornness by tolerance rather than by oppression.

CHAPTER 3

A FESTIVAL OF FAITH AND LIGHT

WHEN the Talmud (*Shabbat* 21b) posits the question מַאי חֲנֻכָּה *Mai Hanukkah?*, the meaning is not 'What is Hanukkah?' but what is its *significance* for all times? It might also have been intended to show that it was an essentially Jewish Festival. The meaning of our annual celebration is that the miracle of Hanukkah repeats itself in each generation, for unceasing is the struggle between those who look upon life as devotion to *beauty*, and those who regard it as a consecration to *duty*. Jewish teaching is adamant in its protest against those who worship the 'Golden Calf' of material possessions, whose delight is a chase after the bizarre, a hankering after the flamboyant.

The occasion of the year when our festival is observed is significant. It is when the days are shortest, the nights longest, the climate far from temperate. It is just at that time that our annual celebration brings the message of hope to all in despair. It is then that we need to be heartened in our belief that the reason of our survival is to be torch-bearers of the art of living together among 'the families of the earth' in peace and goodwill, phrases emphasised at this season by those of the dominant faith. We are forbidden to do work or read

17

by the lights of the Menorah, but to concentrate instead on the tale of martyrdom they evoke.

What appeal for loyalty to Judaism can rival that made by our festival? Hanukkah can only have meaning if its observance results in greater dedication and stauncher championship of our ideals, whatever be the cost of their implementation. This is what the Talmud means when it says: *Hadlakah Osah Mitzvah* (הַדְלָקָה עוֹשָׂה מִצְוָה) it is the *kindling* (in the heart and mind) which is the *real* fulfilment of the observance. Hence the blessing which we recite: '*Blessed art Thou, O Lord our God, King of the Universe who hast hallowed us with His precepts, and who hast commanded us to kindle the lamp of Hanukkah.*'

In the light of the eternal truths with which Jewish teachings have endowed our festival, it is irrelevant to speculate whether Hanukkah is not some relic or adaptation from an ancient pagan ritual. In the course of ages, Judaism may have borrowed from other sources, but it has always suffused these sources with a divine glow all its own.

The fact that the kindling of lights is not mentioned in the Books of the Maccabees is no argument that it was imported from pagan cults, from which also the Christmas tree is said to have originated. In serious scholarship there is a general principle that '*ex silentio, nihil argumentum,*' that proof of non-existence cannot be derived from silence. Incidentally, it is interesting to note that Flavius Josephus (37-95 C.E.) refers to our celebration as the 'Feast of Lights', lights being the symbol of liberation and of the inalienable right of human beings to live and worship in freedom.

The lessons read into Hanukkah must not be taken as belonging to the sphere of homiletics. It is just these interpretations that have given our festival pulsating, colourful, contemporary significance. By being silent on the military triumphs, and concentrating solely on the spiritual victory, the Talmud stressed that the struggle was not so much against oppression from without, as against corruption from within. The Greek invasion was one of ideas, rather than of arms. It was a challenge made by a rich culture which preferred to meet the problems of existence by free philosophy, to a religion based on a codified revelation of God.

Light in Jewish Observance

The celebration of Hanukkah calls attention to the significant place occupied by lights in our faith. It ushered in Creation, its appearance causing chaos to flee. The symbol most favoured in the Bible to express God's Presence, is light. The sun, moon and stars all reflect this heavenly splendour. In Messianic times, the Lord alone will be our everlasting light (*Is.* lx: 19-20). Light came to possess for the Jew spiritual meaning, and served as a convenient symbol of life and joy. 'The soul of man is the lamp of the Lord,' and learning was described by the same symbol. 'For the commandment is a lamp, and the teaching is light.' (*Prov.* vi: 23.)

In post-Biblical literature, wisdom is portrayed as the radiance of the everlasting light of God. Light was one of the first gifts bestowed on Adam, who despaired when night succeeded day, under the impression that he was going to die because of his sin. To allay his fears, God set before him two tiles, from which Adam drew forth sparks of light by striking one against the other. 'Whereupon he blessed God for the light which he thus obtained by his own hands.' (*Gen. R.* xii.) This legend gave birth to the custom of the *Habdalah* ceremony at the termination of the Shabbat when, with tapered candles, spices and wine, we usher in a new week.

Since light was the symbol of joy and spirituality, it gradually became an essential feature whenever the Jew ushered in the annual festival and the weekly Shabbat, or whenever he observed occasions, sad or gay. In the synagogue, the *Ner Tamid* (Perpetual Lamp) reminded him of the everlasting Presence of the 'Guardian of Israel, who neither slumbereth nor sleepeth.' In the words of the Talmud (*Men.* 86b): 'God is in no need of light; the light in the sanctuary was to testify that the light of the Shechinah is in the midst of Israel.' Every synagogue must have windows, unlike the subterranean vault and cloistered monastery of other faiths. In Solomon's Temple (I *Kings* vii), the windows were narrow within but wider towards the exterior to indicate that Judaism floods the outside world with its light.

The reason for this choice of light in the observance of our faith is to remind the Jew that God intended him to be 'a light unto the Gentiles,' whose mission it was to spread spirituality, truth, justice and mercy on earth.

The righteous are referred to as 'the sons of light,' while the wicked are called 'the sons of darkness,' descriptions which have become familiar recently on account of references in the Dead Sea Scrolls.

CHAPTER 4

HASMONEANS AND MACCABEANS

Two words, Hasmoneans and Maccabees, have appeared in these pages with regular frequency. In a popular 'Guide' to our festivals these must receive elucidation. The *Al Ha'Nissim* begins with the words: 'In the days of Mattathias, the son of Johanan, the High Priest, a Hasmonean, and his sons.' Who were the Hasmoneans? It was the family name of the ruling party in Israel in the middle of the second century C.E. It does not appear in the Apocrypha itself, but has come down into the liturgy from Talmudic literature. The Mishnah (*Middoth* i: 6), refers to the Hasmoneans. The story of their rise to power is told in the First Book of the Maccabees. The surname is first associated with Simon Hasmonai, the grandfather of Mattathias, a man of priestly rank and exceeding piety. Some wish to identify the word with a place of that name in the Negev, near Beersheba (*Josh.* xv: 26). Altogether, there were nine rulers of this family, whose power and authority were recognized by the Roman Senate. Herod (10 B.C.E.-44 C.E.) married Mariamne, the last surviving member of this family, only to be responsible for her death, as he was for most who were stumbling-blocks to his ambitions.

The Hasmoneans stand out as conspicuous examples

of patriotism and heroism. "Lovely and pleasant in their lives, in their death they were not divided." Not one of them died a natural death, breathing their last on the gory battlefield. But their supreme sacrifice was not in vain; for thereby they prolonged the lease of life of the Jewish State and gained independence of worship for their co-religionists. Had it not been for them, Judea would have remained a vassal state of the Syrian Empire, and Hellenism would have gained mastery over Judea. Hanukkah is the eternal monument to all they did and dared; their heroic deeds 'shall not fail from among the Jews, nor the memorial of them perish from their seed.'

The Rise and Fall of the Hasmonean Dynasty

The dynasty which began with Simon the Maccabee ended in the dust of inner strife almost a century later. It enjoyed its golden period during the thirty years' reign of John Hyrcanus, who succeeded his illustrious father Simon both as ruler of Judea and High Priest of the Temple in Jerusalem. After Antiochus, King of Syria, who had conquered Judea from Hyrcanus, died in battle against the Parthians, Hyrcanus succeeded in regaining independence. To make sure that this time it would not so easily be lost, he made a treaty of friendship with Rome.

In his zeal both as ruler and High Priest, Hyrcanus conquered Edom, forcing its inhabitants to embrace Judaism; thus making the tragic mistake made by Antiochus who had forced Israel to renounce their ancestral allegiance. Even those whom he had tried most to please—the Pharisees—were determined to depose him from serving as High Priest, in view of some suspicion attached to his birth. The end of his days was marked by strife.

Aristobulus I, the son who succeeded him in 104 B.C.E., was the first of the dynasty to assume the title of King. His reign, marked by leanings towards the Hellenists, lasted one year; during which, according to Josephus, he murdered his mother whom his father had designated to succeed him. The rot which had set into this illustrious family soon spread over the whole country.

His brother Alexander Jannaeus succeeded him as ruler and as husband to his widow, Alexandra Salome. This must have been one of the last instances of levirate marriages (*Yibbum*) recorded in Jewish history. The years during which Jannaeus sat on the Hasmonean throne were characterized by endless warfare. From without against Egypt, Syria and Arabia, implacable foes for all times, it would seem; from within against the Pharisees, at strife always with the ruling powers. Despite this constant state of belligerency, he succeeded to stretch his borders to the extent enjoyed in the palmy days of Solomon. The end of his reign, in 76 B.C.E., was marred by the relentless opposition of the Pharisees, who pelted him during one Sukkot festival with their *Ethrogim*, when he was officiating as High Priest, because he had departed from the traditional prescription for his duties.

It was then that the only other woman (the second being Athaliah, the daughter of Ahab and mother of Ahaziah, whom she succeeded [seventh century B.C.E.]) ever to occupy a Jewish throne as queen, became ruler of Judea. Tradition asserts that she was a sister of R. Simon b. Shetah, the leader of the Pharisees. This explains her constant attempts to placate them. Her death in 67 B.C.E. occasioned a bitter contest for the throne by her two sons Hyrcanus and Aristobulus. Both sought the assistance of foreign powers. Aristobulus climbed to the throne with Roman help, only to be later held as a prisoner in Rome. He was finally poisoned at the hands of an enemy.

The last years of the Hasmonean dynasty are full of blood and fury, signifying hatred. The last nail in their coffin was driven in by Herod the Great (73 B.C.E.- 4 B.C.E.), who murdered his brother-in-law Aristobulus III, the brother of his wife Mariamne. According to legend, when this poor soul could no longer endure the murderous instincts of her royal spouse, she leaped to early death from the palace roof. A voice of heaven (*bat kol*) was heard to cry, as she gasped her last breath 'with Mariamne, the last scion of the Hasmoneans has perished.' A dynasty which began with a trail of glory, ended with a tale of revolts and plots.

The Maccabeans

In the story unfolded by Hanukkah, the Maccabeans are synonymous with the Hasmoneans. It seems a pity that the term is almost exclusively used today to describe prowess in the field of athletics and games. Is the word misused? The best answer is to pass in review the opinions of outstanding scholars as to its precise definition.

The word is nowhere to be found in the Talmud, Midrash, or Liturgy. The earliest reference is in the First Book of the Maccabees (ii: 4), where it describes Judah, one of the five heroic sons of Mattathias, as the Maccabee. It was the Septuagint (LXX) that first called the two Books of the Maccabees by that name. In their desire to Hebraize words of Hellenic origin, Jewish homilists soon discovered that the four Hebrew letters (מ, כ, ב, י) which spelt the word, could be made to yield the initial letters of the four words which comprised the Hasmonean battle-cry 'Who is like unto Thee among the gods, O Lord?' (מִי כָמֹךְ בָּאֵלִים יְ).

Another ingenious explanation is that the word should be pronounced *Mekabbim* (מְכַבִּים), the *extinguishers* of Hellenic persecution. Yet another school of thought suggests that the word describing Judas in I *Macc.* ii: 4 was *Ha'matsbi* (הַמַצְבִּיא) the General, but that in the process of Greek transliteration, the letter *tsaddi* (צ), pronounced by Sephardi Jews to this day as a soft sibilant, came to be pronounced hard, and spelt with a double *c*—Maccabi. The definition usually accepted is that the word was originally spelt with a *Kuph* (ק) and not a *Khaph* (כ), and means 'the hammerer,' from the word *Makkevet* (מַקֶּבֶת) a *hammer*.

Modin, or — ?

The correct spelling of the native town of Mattathias has also been called into question. One scholar, Professor S. Klein, suggests that a more correct pronunciation would be *Modiin* (מוֹדִיעִין). Josephus refers to it as *Modain*, and Eusebius as *Modiim*, with a final *Mem*, the name of a small village near Lydda, (now Israel's famous airport). The name occurs twice in the Mishnah, both as *Modiim* and *Modiit* (*Pes.* ix: 2; *Hagigah* iii: 5). In other texts, notably Palestinian, it appears as *Modiit*. Perhaps both names were then current, but Estoria Ha'Parhi maintains that these were two distinct places. One was called *Modiin*, fifteen miles from Jerusalem, known in Arabic as *Mida'ah*; the other, near Beth She'an, known as *Modait*, or *Madua*.

CHAPTER 5

IN THE APOCRYPHA

Antiochus

'MOREOVER, King Antiochus wrote to his whole Kingdom, that all should be one people. That everyone should leave his laws; all the heathens agreed according to the commandment of the king. Yea, many also of the Israelites consented to his religion, and sacrificed unto idols, and profaned the Sabbath.' (I *Macc.* i: 41-43). The chapter goes on to tell us that all were to build altars on which sacrifices of swine and other animals unclean to Jews were to be offered to the Greek gods. 'That they should leave their children uncircumcised, and make their souls abominable with all manner of profanation. To the end that they might forget the law and change all the ordinances. And whosoever would not do according to the commandment of the King, should die.' (vv. 48-51.)

Many people joined them, namely all who had forsaken the Law. 'Wherever they found any Book of the Testament, or if any consented to the law, the King's commandment was that they be put to death.' (v. 57). 'And on the *twenty-fifth day of the month (Kislev)*, they did sacrifice upon the idol altar, which was upon the altar of God. At which time, according to the commandment, they put to death certain women that had caused their children to be circumcised. Howbeit, many in Israel were fully resolved and confirmed in themselves not to eat of any unclean thing. Wherefore they chose rather to die, that they be not defiled with meats, and that they might not profane the holy covenant: so that they died. And there was great wrath upon Israel.' (vv. 59-64).

The Maccabees (*Precis of* I *Macc*. ii: 1-70)

In those days, did Mattityahu, son of Johanan, move from Jerusalem and settle in Modiim. He had five sons: Johanan, Shimon, Yehudah—called the Maccabi—Elazor and Jonathan. When they beheld the blasphemous things that were done in Judea and Jerusalem, then did Mattityahu and his sons rend their garments, clothe themselves in sackcloth and mourn bitterly. It was now the turn of the officers of the King, whose task it was to enforce the apostasy of the House of Israel, to visit Modiim. When they approached the idol altar there to sacrifice unclean animals, many Israelites joined them.

Mattityahu and his sons observed all this in righteous indignation, and when they witnessed one of their own fellow-Jews boldly step forward, in the eyes of all, to sacrifice swine upon the altar in accordance with the royal command, their ire was kindled. The aged Mattityahu himself, with his zeal for the Lord of Israel giving him wings, rushed forward and slew the Jewish traitor, in front of the altar. He also killed the officer of the King, whose mission had brought him to Modiim in order to compel its inhabitants to sacrifice forbidden things on the altar to Zeus. Pulling down the altar in his fiery wrath, he cried out in a voice loud enough for all to hear: 'Whosoever is zealous of the Law, and maintaineth the covenant, let him follow me' (i: 27).

A company of zealots assembled, ready to do battle with their oppressors. At first they would not fight on the Sabbath day (vv. 31-38), but later it was decided to defend their lives even on that day, if the enemy attacked. 'At that time, therefore, they decreed, saying: "Whoever shall come to make battle with us on the Sabbath day, we will fight against him. Neither will we die all, as our brethren that were murdered in the secret places." ' They were joined by all in whom zeal for the true faith burnt brightly in their hearts, 'mighty men of Israel,' who smote sinful men in their anger, and wicked men in their wrath; but the rest fled to the heathen for succour. (vv. 41-44.)

Re-dedication (*Precis* of I *Macc.* iv)

After their victory, Yehudah the Maccabean, and his brothers, exhorted the people: 'Now that our enemies are crushed, let us go up to purify the Sanctuary, and re-dedicate it.' So the whole army gathered together and went up to Mount Zion. There they purified the sanctuary, pulled down the stone images, broke the altar, and re-built it with unhewn stones, as the Torah requires. The Menorah was re-kindled in a Temple purified and re-dedicated to the true, Eternal God of Israel.

On the morning of the *twenty-fifth* of Kislev, they arose early, offering sacrifices upon the new altar they had made, according to the laws of Moses. This day corresponded to the exact time when the heathen had polluted the Temple and its altar; it was therefore fitting that this day should have been chosen for its re-dedication with song and harp, lute and cymbal. For eight days did this joyous celebration continue, during which they also decorated the forefront of the Temple with crowns of gold and small shields. Amidst much gladness on the part of all, Yehudah and his brothers and all the congregation of Israel solemnly decreed that the days of Hanukkah (re-dedication) should be observed in their season every year for *eight* days, beginning with the *twenty-fifth* of the month of Kislev, and that this festival should always be commemorated with much joy and gladness.

Death of Yehudah, the Maccabean (*Precis* of I *Macc*. ix)

And Yehudah was encamped at Elasa, and had three thousand picked men with him. When they saw how numerous were the forces against them, they were greatly terrified and many slipped away from the army. In all, not more than 800 men were left. When Yehudah saw that his army melted away, while the battle was imminent, he was troubled in his heart, having no time to rally them. In desperation, he exhorted those who had loyally remained with him: 'Let us arise and attack our enemies; perhaps we may prevail against them.'

They replied: 'This we cannot do now in view of the paucity of our members. Would it not be better to save our lives now, returning later with increased forces to wage battle against them.'

Yehudah replied: 'Heaven forbid that I should do such a thing—and flee from my enemies! If our time has come, then let us die manfully for our noble cause. Why stain with reproach the glory once ours?'

So they advanced against the hosts of the enemy, and the battle raged the whole day long, from morning until evening. Now Yehudah saw that the main flanks of Bacchides and Alcimus—which comprised 20,000 footmen and 2,000 horsemen and were stationed at Berea—were on the right wing. The reward of his military strategy and prowess was to see the enemy beaten back and inviting pursuit. And when those on the left wing saw the plight of their own side, they turned upon Yehudah's men from behind. The pendulum now began to swing desperately against the Jewish army. On both sides the casualties were heavy, but the Jews suffered worst of all; for Yehudah fell in battle, and the rest fled.

Then did Jonathan and Shimon take their brother Yehudah and buried him in the tomb of his fathers at Modiim. And they bewailed him there, with all Israel weeping and mourning for him many days long. The lament taken up was: 'How are the mighty fallen, the saviour of Israel!' At that time, Jonathan took the leadership upon him in the place of his fallen brother Yehudah.

CHAPTER 6

IN THE HALACHA

THIS chapter contains a synopsis of the laws regulating the celebration of Hanukkah according to the Talmud and the Codes.

The lights should be kindled each evening, from the *twenty-fifth* of *Kislev,* and placed near the door or window, where passers-by will be able to observe them. In so doing, the miracle will be proclaimed far and wide. It is meritorious to dispense charity to those in need, especially those engaged in study of the Torah.

Being a festival, it should be honoured with good food, during the enjoyment of which *zemirot* should be sung, and the story of the Maccabean victory related to the children and guests around the table. Fasting is not allowed; except in the days preceding and following when it is. Work is permitted, though it is customary for women not to work in the house while the lights burn. The greater stringency on the part of women is because the Maccabees saved them from the degradation imposed upon Jewish brides by the Syrian-Greeks on the eve of their marriage; also because of the miracle performed by Judith in depriving the Greek general Holofernes of his head thus hastening victory for Israel.

All kinds of oil may be used, yet pure olive-oil should be preferred, for the miracle occurred with the

C

sealed cruse of olive-oil. Candles used for Christmas trees and at non-Jewish festivals should not be used, nor should those that produce several flames joined together, such as the plaited tapers used for *Habdalah*. Each flame should be distinct. Some authorities declare that lights produced by electricity or gas may not be used. If they are, the prescribed benediction may not be made.

It is desirable that each household member light his own candles, for it is a *Mitzvah* imposed on individuals, be they women or minors. The lights should not be placed at the usual place of the lamp, for that would blur the distinction of the celebration. In olden times, and also in more clement climates, the *Menorah* used to be placed outside the house for all to see. When hostility against Jews became prevalent, they were removed in order to grace the inside of the home.

It is usual to place the *Menorah* on the *left* of the door leading to the street, facing the *Mezuzah* on the right. Thus he who enters the house will be flanked by two great *mitzvot*, to the right and left of him. Care should be taken to place the lights neither too high nor too low, so as to ensure that their presence does not escape the eye. The proper time for their kindling is when three stars appear in the sky. When this time approaches, no work, not even study, should be engaged in; but the evening prayer (*ma'ariv*) may be recited. In cases of emergency, the lighting may take place either before or after this stipulated time.

Before kindling the lights, the head of the household should assemble all its members in honour of the celebration. Enough oil must be put into the *Hanukkiyah* (lamp), or the candles must be sufficiently large to last at least half-an-hour after the stars have appeared. Should they not burn so long, the *mitzvah* has not been properly fulfilled.

The lights in the Menorah should be kindled from the left, proceeding to the right. Three benedictions are recited on the first night; the blessing over the kindling, that over the miracle and the third (to be omitted after the initial night), in which gratitude is expressed to the Almighty for enabling us to reach this day. After the blessings, the lights are kindled, and the paragraph *Ha'nerot Ha'lalu* recited.

When placing the lights in position near the open door or window, care should be taken that they be not blown out. If this precaution be neglected, they must be re-kindled, without the blessings; but if all possible care were exercised, and still they were extinguished before the stipulated time for their burning, the obligation has been fulfilled. They should, however, be re-kindled without the usual blessing. During the half-hour which is the minimum time they must burn, no use may be made of their light for reading, work, or any other purpose. Since prevention is better than cure, the custom prevails of having an extra candle, called a *Shammash* (servitor), so that if by any chance one does read or do any work by the light of the *Menorah*, this can be ascribed to the light cast by the *Shammash*, and not by the 'holy lights.' To distinguish this light from the others, it is placed in another row by itself.

During the *Shivah* (שִׁבְעָה) (week of mourning), the mourner lights the candles at home, with the *She'he'yanu* (שֶׁהֶחֱיָנוּ) benediction. This blessing he is precluded from making in synagogue if he happens to conduct the first evening service of Hanukkah.

On the eve of Shabbat, the Hanukkah lamp is kindled before the Shabbat lights, for the reverse process would mean kindling lights after the Shabbat has begun. At the end of the Shabbat, the *habdalah* precedes the kindling of the Hanukkah lights at home; in the synagogue, they are kindled before reciting *Ve'yitten Lecha*. (וְיִתֶּן לְךָ).

The *Al-ha'nissim* paragraph is inserted in the *Amidah* and Grace after meals throughout the festival. The *complete* version of the Hallel is added to the morning liturgy. All supplicatory prayers, like *Tahanun*, Psalm xx, and others of a similar nature, are omitted. Three persons are called up on each of the weekdays to the Scriptural reading from *Numbers* vii: 1-54—viii: 14. On the Shabbat, two Scrolls of the Law are taken from the Ark; from one the weekly Sidra is read, from the other the special Scriptural portion of Hanukkah. The *Haphtarah* is from *Zech.* ii: 14—iv: 7. Should there be another Shabbat during the festival, the *Haphtarah* is from Kings which describes the Menorah made by Solomon.

If the month of Tebet begins on a weekday, two Scrolls are used. To the first, three persons are called, to whom the portion relevant to Rosh Hodesh (*Num.* xxviii: 2-15) is read; to the fourth person is read the portion referring to the festival. The reason according to the Talmud, is that precedence is given to that which occurs more often; Hanukkah comes once, whereas the New Moon occurs twelve times in an ordinary year.

Should the New Moon of Tebet occur on a Shabbat, *three* Scrolls are used. To the first, six persons are called to whom the current weekly Sidra is read; to the second, the seventh person is called for the reading of the passage of Rosh Hodesh, but starting from *Num.* xxviii: 9-15; the half Kaddish is recited, after which the portion relevant to the festival is read as Maphtir from the third Scroll. The reason for the three Scrolls is the obligation 'to *proclaim* the miracle' (לְפַרְסוּמֵי נִסָּא).

CHAPTER 7

IN THE SYNAGOGUE

THE liturgy for the festival has been edited to reflect its joyous nature, all prayers of supplication tinged with sadness being omitted. The lights are kindled before the evening (*ma'ariv*) service, beginning with one and culminating with a crescendo of light and song on the eighth night. The fleeting glimpse of the Maccabean message, caught on the first eve of the festival, must become an abiding vision.

Why Lights in the Synagogue?

Hanukkah is essentially a home celebration. The public kindling was intended to serve as a reminder of the number of lights to be kindled that evening at home. Many authorities like Abraham Ha'Yarhi (*Ha'manhig* clix), and R. Ephraim (*Shibalei Ha'leket* clxxiv) questioned the wisdom of the synagogue celebration; their contention being that it was purely a domestic observance. R. Joseph Karo (*Beth Joseph*), as well as the compiler of the *Kol Bo*, argue in favour of its celebration in the synagogue because of the wayfarers who were given board there in times gone by. The *Kiddush* was recited in the synagogue, as well as in the home, on the eve of Shabbat and Yomtov for this reason.

Where there was no *quorum* of ten male adults (*minyan*), the benedictions were omitted in the synagogue. The lights had to be kindled at home, although this had already been witnessed in the synagogue. They were re-kindled, without a blessing, in the morning. For this, there are two reasons. It helps 'to proclaim the miracle' if they are kindled at an unusual time and secondly it is a reminder to those who had accidentally forgotten to light the lights at home.

Supplementary Prayers

In the *Amidah*, the *Al-Ha'nissim* is added, describing succinctly the festival story from the origin of the struggle till its triumphant sequel. The *Hallel* is recited daily, as well as a special Scriptural portion from *Numbers* vii: 1-54—viii: 4. The *Haphtarah* on the Shabbat is from *Zech.* ii: 14—iv: 7, wherein occurs the declaration 'Not by might, and not by strength, but by My Spirit, said the Lord of hosts.'

It is apposite that the festival should be singled out for honour in the synagogue—the bastion of Jewish idealism. Time could perhaps be found for supplementing the synagogue service further on this Shabbat by a public reading of passages from the Books of the Maccabees. The *Al-Ha'nissim* passage concludes with the reminder that following their victory, the Hasmoneans 'entered the inner sanctuary of Thy House, cleansed the Temple, purified Thy holy place, and kindled lights in Thy sacred courts.' The purification of the Temple took pride of place over their homes.

No *Megillah* is recited on Hanukkah. During the Middle Ages the Scroll of Antiochus or the Hasmoneans was read in Italian synagogues; it is done among Yemenite Jews to this day. Sa'adia Gaon (882-942) attributed its authorship to the five sons of Mattathias. The consensus of scholarly opinion is that it is a product of the seventh century c.e., originally composed in Aramaic, the Hebrew version being a translation. As is inevitable across the ages, some customs dropped whilst others were added.

The Ma'oz Tsur

If the initial letters of the five paragraphs, which comprise this spirited hymn, can serve as an indication of its authorship, its composer must have been one called Mordecai (מָרְדְּכַי). A device favoured by medieval hymnologists was to weave their names into poems. We know little about this Mordecai, save that he lived in the thirteenth century.

The tune to which it has been popularly wedded is believed to be an adaptation of a German song about three hundred years old. So excellently does it match the spirit of the festival that the Maccabees themselves might have hummed it as they marched into battle. Its five stanzas record the miraculous Exodus from Egypt, the Babylonian exile, the rise and fall of Haman, and the resounding victory of the Maccabeans.

Next to the *Hatikvah* itself, the *Ma'oz Tsur* is probably the best-known melody among Jews the world over. Majesty and daring are its *leit-motifs*, and it echoes the hope and confidence with which the Maccabeans marched into battle. The tune was adopted by Martin Luther to one of his hymns, probably importing it direct from a German lyric of the fifteenth century to which it was first sung. Though the hymn was no doubt originally intended for home jollification it was good to have introduced it into the synagogue service. For only when life is introduced into our synagogue can its influence be introduced into daily life and thought.

CHAPTER 8

IN THE JEWISH HOME

THE synagogue service reflects the nature of Hanukkah, essentially a festival for the home. It was from homes in which the simple pieties were observed, that the Maccabeans drew their strength. The kindling of the lights, when labour's task was done and the entire family grouped around the officiating father, and the chanting of the lilting melody of *Ma'oz Tsur* etherealize the Jewish home into a palace of holiness and happiness. It is largely the home celebration which converts Hanukkah into a festival of unforgettable heroism, recalling those mighty souls who caught whispers of eternal things and bequeathed them as a legacy of their indomitable spirit. Surrounded by those we love, and who love us, we regard with affectionate admiration those souls who, by their unyielding demands for right conduct and moral living, arrested the paralysing influences of their day. The souls of the Hasmoneans shine like beacon-lights, flooding the dark valley of the years with their blaze of glory.

It is not without significance that the same root from which the Hebrew word Hannukkah is derived, also supplies the word for education (חִנּוּךְ) and for the consecration or dedication of a new home (חֲנֻכַּת הַבַּיִת). A sound Jewish education, or a complete

Hasmonean-like loyalty to Judaism, can be fed by the home-fires of pious example and virtuous living. History, Jewish and non-Jewish, is replete with instances of the effects upon a nation if its home-life is endangered. To cite the example from the two other nations—Greece and Rome—which, together with Israel, made weighty contributions to civilization. The Greek historian Thucydides, in his history of the Peloponnesian Wars, bewails that the Athenians no longer practise in their homes the moral pieties of their ancestors. He warns his contemporaries: 'We shall be utterly destroyed, because we have destroyed our home-life.' That he prophesied correctly, subsequent events proved only too well.

A similar fate befell Rome, as well as nations nearer our own day who have allowed the religious structure of their homes to be dissolved. Observances in the home, like those of Hanukkah, enable the parent to impart to his child during its most impressionable years, the beauty of a life lived according to Jewish teachings. The festival lights of Hanukkah should make parents aware of their responsibilities clearly, and not as in a vision, darkly.

Why Games are Played

In view of the attitude adopted by our Talmudic sages towards games of chance, such as card-playing or dice throwing, disqualifying those who habitually indulge in them from acting as witnesses in Jewish

Courts of Law, it may seem surprising that card-playing on Hanukkah has become almost traditional. The following explanation may be conjectural, yet one not devoid of plausibility. Owing to the decree of Antiochus, which forbade the study of the Torah, enforcing this harsh measure by the dispatch of inspectors to homes suspected of disobedience, recourse was had to subterfuge. While engaged in the study of their Holy Books, alone or with their friends, they had at hand a pack of cards dealt out before each student, ready to play with them when the need arose.

The *Trendle*—on the four sides of which were engraved the letters, *nun, gimmel, he, shin*, each given their respective numerical value of 50, 3, 5, 300, and made to be the initial letters of the words נֵס גָּדוֹל הָיָה שָׁם 'a great miracle took place there,' served as *an alibi*. In the event of being caught studying, they could plead that they were enjoying a friendly game of chance. Fanciful, it is true; yet if the cards and the *trendle* saved the study of Judaism from jeopardy, they will be remembered in gratitude by future generations.

It has also been surmised that games were played since no study, reading or work of any sort was allowed when the lights were burning. Such customs, provided they contribute towards the serenity of the home and the feelings of concord which should prevail among its members, deserve to be woven into the pattern of Jewish folk-ways. Jews, on the whole, have not been encouraged by Rabbinic authorities to devote much time to sports, not because Judaism is against such exercises, but because these would mean a lessening of the precious hours which should be devoted to the undisturbed pursuit of Torah-study in which we are told 'to meditate day and night.'

CHAPTER 9

A FESTIVAL LINKED WITH ETERNITY

WE shall have failed if we have not made it clear that Hanukkah is unique as a national observance, not only because the stage of the struggle was actually on Jewish soil, while all other anniversaries have alien stages, but also because it is essentially religious, free from propaganda of a patriotic or party bias. This aspect is implicit in the reason Mattathias gave for his rebellion against the tyranny of Antiochus. This was *not* to regain the political independence of Judea—an independence it hardly had since its restoration by Cyrus of Persia—but to re-establish the freedom of religious worship of which Antiochus had robbed them. Mattathias told the King's officer who came to bribe him to forsake Judaism: 'We will not hearken to the King's words to go from our religion either to the right hand, or to the left.' Under his banner, he rallied men of valour, like Gideon of old, who were of his calibre—staunch and religious. His battle-cry was: 'Whoever is for God, follow me!'

We have already indicated that it was primarily the religious persecution of Antiochus Epiphanes which whipped the more devout element to revolt. While not repudiating political allegiance, it was essentially a struggle against abuses in the realm of faith. Let us be clear on this point: *it is the dedication of the Temple and the restoration of the sacrificial cult, rather than the renewal of political independence which is the crux of the festival.* Such was the motive of Hanukkah observance throughout the ages, and such the spirit in which it was commemorated. It was never meant as a feast glorifying the triumph of statehood. To obliterate the part played by the Divine in the struggle and to boast of the prowess of Jewish might is to forget the warning of Deuteronomy, that one should not say that it was 'the power and might of my hand which hath gotten me this wealth; but thou shalt remember the Lord thy God, for it is He that giveth you power to get wealth.'

It would be wrong to ignore the fact that the military successes engendered a movement for political independence as well. Subsequent events were favourable. For in 142 B.C.E., Simon, the last of the Maccabee brothers, severed the final bonds of allegiance to the Syrian rulers and succeeded in obtaining the withdrawal of the Greek garrison from the Acra, the fortress dominating the approach to Jerusalem. He began to strike his own coins, the first ever to be issued by a Jewish state and the sure sign of complete independence. It is this Hasmonean dynasty which is described as ruling the Second Jewish State.

Sad to relate, this monarchy was not of very long duration. The internal, intensive quarrels between members of the Hasmonean dynasty led to alien interference when the Roman general Pompey invaded Palestine and captured Jerusalem. The Second Jewish

Commonwealth met with disaster in the year 70 C.E., only to be revived again on the Fifth of Iyar, 5708.

The Hope of Immortality

The truths proclaimed by the flickering lights of Hanukkah will never be extinguished. We may say a thousand times: 'My soul and conscience, be silent! I want my physical comfort,' but human nature being what it is, faith will fire our conscience and point mockingly to our own folly. The spirit which is Hanukkah will ever gird the Jew with strength to snatch the palm of victory from those who plot his extermination. True to his inner sense of proportion, the pious Jew will never allow the festival to be debased into a military tattoo, a trooping of the colours, and a display of martial power. To him, the name Maccabee conjures up visions of brave souls to whom 'the dew of heaven' was preferable to 'the fat things of the earth.'

The festival will live because of the new note it struck in Jewish belief—a hope in immortality. The bravery for martyrdom was intensified by the glow of the belief in the Life to Come. The second of the seven sons of Hannah (all of whom preferred martyrdom to apostasy), in his spirited refusal to obey the king's command to renounce his faith in the God of Israel, spoke thus: 'Thou, like a fury, takest us out of this present life; but the King of the world shall raise us up who have died for his laws, unto everlasting life.' (II *Macc*. vii: 9). The fourth son spoke likewise: 'It is good, being put to death by men, to look for hope from

48

God to be raised up again by Him. As for thee (O King), thou shalt have no resurrection to life.' (*ibid.* v: 14). The seventh and youngest of the brothers crowned and sealed his earthly life with this declaration: 'For our brethren, who now have suffered a short pain, our dead under God's covenant of everlasting life. But thou, through the judgment of God, shalt receive just punishment for thy pride.' (*ibid.* v: 36).

D

PART II

PURIM

CHAPTER I

THE STORY

THE best synopsis cannot serve as a substitute for the Purim story vividly told in the Book of Esther, a story which must be read in its entirety—preferably in its Hebrew original—to be enjoyed. The dramatic intensity of this popular romance, the characters of which are sketched with consummate skill, will repay the time thus spent.

The scene opens with the banquet held by Ahasuerus, whose empire extended over 120 provinces, ranging from India to Ethiopia. To this magnificent feast nobles and princes were invited, before whom luxurious dishes and rare wines were spread. When the festivities reached their height and the influence of the wine began to be felt, the King ordered Vashti to appear before that vast assembly arrayed in all her beauty. This the queen refused to do. She was deposed, and a search instituted for a new consort.

The Purim story begins with the selection of Esther, a mysterious Jewess from nowhere, who charmed the

Emperor with her natural beauty and innate dignity. She was accompanied to the Palace by her kinsman Mordecai, a loyal Jew who refused to bend the knee to Haman, one of the ministers bloated to inordinate vanity by the power vested in him by the Emperor. Mordecai learned of the devilish plot of Haman who, incensed by his refusal to pay him the obeissance reserved only for his God, persuaded the King to authorise the destruction of all the Jews in his Kingdom whom he accused of rebelliousness. To support his cause, Haman offered the King a huge sum of money with which to fill the coffers of the Palace that would need replenishing after the Jews were no more. Mordecai entreated Esther to plead with the King to nullify this decree, at the same time warning her that if she refused so to do, salvation would come 'from another quarter'—a reference to God. Though at first daunted by the task, Esther finally decided on a plan as ingenious as it was successful. She would invite both the King and Haman to a banquet in her own private apartments.

It flattered the conceit of both men, not least Haman, to be entertained by a queen to whom mystery lent enchantment. At this banquet she requested that both the King and Haman accept her invitation to the next banquet in their honour. Before the second banquet the sleep of the King was disturbed, and he sought his scribes to read unto him his Book of Chronicles. There it was recorded that Mordecai, the Jew, had frustrated the plot of Bigthan and Teresh. When the King learned that Mordecai had not yet been rewarded for this loyal act he gave orders for this to be remedied immediately.

Haman was commanded by the King to have Mordecai robed in royal apparel, driven on a handsome steed through the main streets of Shushan and to proclaim for all to hear: 'Thus shall it be done to a man whom the King delighteth to honour.' Haman had hardly pocketed his pride after this unexpected turn of events, when the second banquet in Esther's apartments took place. At this banquet Esther unmasked the plans of Haman. The King's wrath was aroused and the authority, vested hitherto in Haman, was handed over to Mordecai. Salvation had come. The last chapters record the *crescendo* of joy and feasting which followed the revenge taken upon those who had sought to exterminate them. As a permanent reminder of the divine deliverance, Mordecai and Esther instituted Purim as a National Festival to be annually commemorated on the Fourteenth Day of Adar, the following day to be known as Shushan Purim.

Its Date

Ahasuerus is identified usually with the Persian King Xerxes (486–465 B.C.E.), though the Septuagint mistakes him for Artaxerxes, his successor. The question of the date has occasioned difficulties, chief of which being that if Mordecai was one of the exiles carried to Babylon in 597 (B.C.E.)—as is stated in ii: 6—he must have been about 120 years old in the reign of Xerxes when the story opens. Similarly Esther, an orphan whom he had brought up from childhood, could not have been very much younger—rather a hard pill to swallow in view of the glamour attached to her. Moreover, the names of Mordecai and Esther are not in the list of the famous men praised in Ecclesiasticus (Ben Sira) xliv-l. In fact, the earliest reference to the Purim story outside the Bible, is found in the Second Book of the Maccabees (xv: 36), a work usually assigned to the year 120 B.C.E. There we read of 'Mordecai's Day' following 'Nicanor's Day,' observed on Adar the thirteenth. From the Talmud, which devotes an entire Tractate to Purim (*Megillah*), we learn that it was the Synod of Jammia (Jabneh), round about the year 90 C.E., which included the Book of Esther in the Biblical canon— thanks largely to the persuasive authority of Rabbi Akiba. It was the profound sense of the indestructibility of Israel and the duty of the Jew to maintain the cause of his people at whatever risk—as Mordecai and Esther did—that was primarily responsible for its retention. This reason is preferable to the one advanced by Biblical critics: that the purpose of the Book is to provide justification for the continued celebration of a festival which had no religious significance or basis in the Torah, but which had become popular among Jews. In the next chapter we shall endeavour to show that though difficulties do abound no alternative theory as to its date, origin and purpose has, so far, proved convincing.

The Name Purim

From the *Megillah* it would appear that this was a Persian word meaning '*lots.*' Owing to its unfamiliarity to the general Jewish reader, the Hebrew equivalent *goral* had to be given. Scholars of Persian literature assure us that no such word has been found and that the history of Persia knows no Mordecai, Esther or Vashti. Assyrian archæologists have come to the rescue. On a votive tablet, of which hundreds have been found in Tel-el-Amarna, has been found the word *purru*, which connotes a 'stone' or 'dice,' in a phrase transcribed to mean 'he shall cast his lots' (*purru*). Such arguments and discoveries do little to discredit the authenticity of a Book which has given joy to countless generations of Jews, to whom joyous faith gave strength to survive the plots for their extermination.

CHAPTER 2

HISTORY—OR MYTH?

ALMOST everything about the vivid and dramatic story has been declared by Bible critics to belong to myth. It is said that the events which it colourfully narrates never occurred, and that characters as Esther, Mordecai, Vashti or Haman never existed. With these denigrations in mind, it is pertinent to consider whether or not there is any historical basis for the festival.

Some of the Objections

With a learning as profound as any of the devastating critics, Prof. J. Hoschander (*The Book of Esther in the Light of History*, Philadelphia, 1923) has dealt with the criticisms. His refutations are convincing and authentic. To summarise his inferences will enable us to draw our own conclusions.

One of the objections is that the story does not occur in Persian historical records. But an *argumentum ex silentio* (an argument from silence) is hardly conclusive. May not these Persian records have been deliberately destroyed in view of the Jewish miraculous triumph? On the other hand, what other people has exercised such a faithful vigil over their holy books as the Jews, who fast when a *Sepher Torah* is accidentally dropped and who kiss the *Siddur* or *Humash* when it falls to the ground? It might well be that the Persians did not consider this local episode important enough to transmit it to posterity. The number of over 75,000 Persians slain (ix: 15-17) might be an hyperbole, of which figure-of-speech the ancients were fond.

Internal evidence has proved an obstacle to many of the authenticity of the Book. Though the Midrash tries hard to Hebraize the names of Mordecai and Esther, the critics cling to the view that these names portray *Marduk* and *Ishtar*, two of the deities in the pantechnicon of Eastern idols. In the LXX (Septuagint), continue the denigrators, the festival is called *fruria*, and no mention is made of the word Purim, 'lots.' One of their criticisms is that the historical dates are hopelessly mixed up. Thus it is stated (ii: 5-6) that Mordecai, the great grandson of Kish, 'a Benjammite, who had been carried away with Jeconiah, King of Judah, whom Nebuchadnezzar, the King of Babylon, had carried away.' Since the Exile took place in 598 B.C.E., and the story of Purim occurred between 485-465 B.C.E., this would make Mordecai a man of about 130 years old—an age considered far too old even in those remote days of long ago.

To this objection, two answers have been advanced. One: that the words *'who had been carried away'* refer not to Mordecai but to Kish, his great-grandfather. Two: that the Ahasuerus of our story is not Xerxes, but Artaxerxes II, who reigned about a century later (403-358 B.C.E.). The description of this Sultan in Herodotus as one who loved wine, women and war tallies closely with the description of him in Esther. Who can gainsay Hoschander's conclusion that 'in view of our scant knowledge about the history of ancient Persia, our failure to identify these events and characters cannot invalidate the story told by one who lived much nearer to the events, and who was acquainted with the circumstantial details'? It has been suggested that the author was Mordecai himself. Talmudic opinion attributes its authorship to the 'Men of the Great Assembly,' the central authority for all matters Jewish in the fifth and fourth centuries B.C.E. (*B. Bath.* 15a; *Meg.* 2a).

The Missing Link

On strictly pious grounds, the authenticity of the Book has been questioned because the Name of God is significantly absent. This omission may have been intentional, for the story pulsates with faith in God throughout. A sense of Divine Providence pervades all the *dramatis personæ*, especially Mordecai and Esther (see iv: 14). In fact, the slogan of the Book seems to be that, '*the Guardian of Israel neither slumbereth, nor sleepeth*' (*Psalms* cxxi: 4). According to Abraham ibn Ezra, the Name was deliberately omitted as a precaution; for in case of a Persian translation, the Name of God would be altered to that of some Persian idol.

It has been suggested that the Divine Name might be uttered with irreverence when under the influence of the wine and conviviality of a festival whose secularity tends to eclipse its essentially spiritual nature. It can be argued that the fact that the deliverance is not attributed directly to God is evidence that Purim was an actual historical event told in a convincing and unadorned style. The burden of the Book is that 'God moves in a mysterious way His manifold wonders to perform' and that He *does* intervene to save His people in every generation, but that He does so through human instruments (Cf. *Isa.* x: 1).

The discussion recorded in the Talmud (*Meg.* 7a), in which the Men of the Great Assembly at first refused, but eventually conceded, to institute the festival as an everlasting memorial, was due not to the absence of God from its records, nor even to its so-called pagan origin, but to other reasons. There was the rooted objection, as in the case of Hanukkah, of glamorizing military victory or miraculous deliverance at the cost of lives. Judaism warns us not to rejoice at the downfall of an enemy. Perhaps the main reluctance is voiced in a passage in the Talmud *Jerushalmi* (*Meg.* ci) '85 elders were very sad about this affair. They said: "Moses told us: 'No prophet should add anything from now and henceforth'; yet Mordecai and Esther desire to appoint a new institution." But they ceased not to ponder over it, until God opened their eyes and they found a justification for it within the Law, the Prophets and the Writings.'

Objection may have been due to the fact that the Rabbis were not in favour of introducing convivial festivals which might be patterned on the carnivals of the heathens. Reluctance may have at first been shown to the 'Persianization' of Esther and Mordecai to resemble the two national deities. That the Rabbis relented and admitted the Book into the Biblical canon, finally proclaiming Purim as a national festival, is further proof of the proverb that '*Vox populi, vox Dei*,' (The Voice of the People is the Voice of God). Hearing the Megillah read in the synagogue was ruled obligatory on man, woman and child; and *gift-giving* was declared an essential part of the celebration.

An Eternal Festival

Having examined several arguments of the critics, we can understand the categorical statement in Talmud and Midrash that the festival will, like the Jews themselves, exhaust Eternity. Poet and philosopher join in acclaiming Purim as eternal. 'And that these days should be remembered and kept throughout every generation; and that these days of Purim should not fail from among the Jews, nor the memorial of them perish from their seed.' (*Esther* ix: 28). 'Whereas all other festivals will one day (in the Messianic era) be outmoded, Purim will always survive' (Midrash to Proverbs ix). The voice of the hymnologist joins in this pæan in the poem added to the liturgy of *Parshat Zakhor* (פַּרְשַׁת זָכוֹר) (the Shabbat preceding Purim). The authoritative opinion of Maimonides is: 'Though all memory of other sorrows in our national history may be dimmed and forgotten, the days of Purim never will' (*Hil. Meg.* ii: 8).

Though the earliest mention of Purim as a fixed observance occurs in the Maccabean age (second century B.C.E.), it cannot be argued that it originated then in order to commemorate the victory over the Syrian-Greeks. Nor is it a Persian tale, retold with a Jewish colouration. It was already established before 70 C.E., for the priests officiating in the Temple were told to brush aside sacrificial duties to listen to the reading of the Megillah (*Meg.* 3b). To sum up: Whatever the origin of Purim may have been, whether these were Persian orgies accompanying the New Year, or the Bacchanalean revels of the Greek-Syrian period, no festival has been suffused with such glow and sanctity.

CHAPTER 3

IN THE HALACHA

It is fallacious to regard the laws of Judaism as attempts at formalism, rendering stereotyped and mechanical that which should be purely ethical and moral. On the contrary, the aim of the *Halacha* is to make the evanescent habitual, and the passing emotion an abiding vision. The laws of Purim, as indeed all those found in our Codes, are not intended to commemorate revenge, vindictiveness and the downfall of our enemies, but to keep ever-green in our minds the hope of the ultimate triumph of that which is just. Their aim is to foster the unshakable belief that 'the Eternal One of Israel does not falsify or disappoint.' (I *Sam.* xv: 29.)

The Public Reading of the Megillah

At the end of the fast on the thirteenth of Adar, in memory of the three-day fast which Esther proclaimed (iv: 16), the Megillah is read immediately following the evening (*Ma'ariv*) service. Before its reading, it is customary to give half-a-*shekel* (usually half-a-crown) for division among the poor. This is reminiscent of the half-*shekel* collected in Adar in Temple times, for the purchase of congregational sacrifices. Some are prompted to give three such coins in view of the fact that the word *Terumah* (תְּרוּמָה) (offering) occurs thrice in *Exodus* xxx: 11-16, the passage read on *Parshat Shekalim* (פָּרָשַׁת שְׁקָלִים), the special Shabbat ushering in Adar.

All are required to hear the reading—men, women and children. This public reading occurs in the evening, after the three stars had appeared, and again in the morning, when dawn has flushed the sky. Should one be unable to attend synagogue through illness or any other cause the Megillah may be read at home. The study of the Torah may be interrupted for this reading; there being no other religious duty for which the Megillah can be postponed except that of burying the dead, if there be none else to attend to that. It is the custom for the Reader to spread out the Scroll prior to the reading, as if it were a *Dispatch* which he has just received. *In the Book of Esther*, the Megillah is referred to as *iggeret* (letter, or dispatch) (ix: 26). It is related of R. Joshua b. Levi that he used to assemble the members of his family to read the Megillah to them.

To initiate children into Jewish observance, they were brought into the synagogue for the reading. Babes in arms, who might disturb the service for each word to be followed, were not to be brought. It may have been that the custom of stamping with the feet or the turning of the *gregger* (see Chap. IV *A Purim Glossary*) whenever Haman was mentioned, as well as the loud repetition by the congregation of certain verses, were devices to keep the children alert from start to finish. The pronunciation of the names of Haman's ten sons in one breath may also have been due to this reason. For this custom two other reasons have been usually advanced. One is that they were all hanged together; the other, the ethical reminder not to gloat over the downfall of an enemy necessitated a hurried glossing over their sad end.

The Megillah may be read when standing or sitting. Out of respect for the congregation it should be read standing. Three blessings are recited before the reading and one at the conclusion. One should use a Megillah written with the care of a *Sepher Torah* itself. Where no such Megillah exists a printed Bible will do. In that contingency the blessings are omitted. The law frowns upon reading it from memory for the obligation is not thereby fulfilled. One who does not understand Hebrew also fulfils his obligation, since it is taken as 'read' that he knows the purport of the story. It is advisable to have the Book of Esther at the Service in order to follow each word in an undertone.

A mourner during his *shivah* on Purim should observe the laws of mourning, though he is permitted publicly to discard signs of grief. He may attend synagogue to hear the *Megillah* and to send gifts to his friends, but these should not be of a joyful nature. To a mourner one should not send gifts during the first year, unless he be poor. In such a case, or if he be the only other Jew in the place, it is permitted to do so in order to fulfil the precept of sending portions, so that it be not forgotten as an established custom in Israel.

The Feast of Purim

It is obligatory to eat, drink and be merry on Purim. One does not fulfil his obligation with the feast at night, for the Megillah refers to '*days* of rejoicing.' It is proper to light candles even when the meal is in broad daylight, for joy should be accompanied by light. 'Unto the Jews, there was light and joy' (viii: 16). It is well to engage in study of Torah before the meal, for 'light' refers to the Torah, a pre-requisite to every sensation of joy.

During the morning service, and before the recital of the Megillah, nine Scriptural verses are read. (*Ex.* xvii: 8-16.) The passage begins with the words: 'And Amalek came'—a reminder of the genealogy of Haman, who, according to tradition, was a scion of Amalek. The reading of the *Maphtir* and *Haphtarah* on the Sabbath preceding (*Parshat Zakhor*) from *Deut.* xxv: 17 and I *Samuel* xv respectively, is a further reminder of Haman's pedigree.

One of the features of Purim is the bestowal of alms. Says Maimonides (*Hil. Meg.* ii: 17): 'It is better for a man to be generous in his gifts to the poor than to be generous in the provision he makes for his Purim meal, and in the presents he intends sending to his intimate friends. There can be no nobler joy than to rejoice the heart of the poor, the orphan, widow and stranger; for he who makes them to rejoice is following the Divine pattern of "reviving the spirit of the humble, and refreshing the heart of those contrite." ' (*Isa.* lvii:15).

E

Work, though permitted on Purim, should be avoided. No blessing results therefrom, unless such be necessary for Purim itself, or is an essential duty that does not require undue effort. Wedding ceremonies are not performed, on the principle that 'one should not intermingle one joyous event with another' (אֵין מְעָרְבִין שִׂמְחָה בְּשִׂמְחָה). Such a mingling is bound to minimize the joy of each; for 'everything that is too much, often spells something else diminished,' a Talmudic Rabbi shrewdly observes. (*Moed Katan.*)

The *Fifteenth* of Adar is called *Shushan* Purim, because of the fighting which continued there on the fourteenth, and from which they rested on the fifteenth (ix: 18). We observe Shushan Purim to this day as a semi-festival, beginning the Purim feast (*Seudah*) on the afternoon of the fourteenth and prolonging it till well in the evening of the fifteenth. Since the Megillah is not read on that day, the joy is less than that which prevailed on the preceding day, hence marriages are allowed. The Hallel is not recited on Purim for several reasons. First: since the Megillah contains praises of God for His miracles, by implication if not expressly, the *Hallel* was considered redundant. Second: the Talmud asks, 'Why rejoice to the full with Hallel, when we are still the slaves of the Ahashverots?'

In the Liturgy
Though the liturgy does not include *Hallel*, reference is made to the festival by the inclusion of

Al Ha'nissim (עַל־הַנִּסִּים) in the *Amidah* and Grace. This is a comprehensive summary of the Purim story. 'Then in Shushan, the capital city, in the time of Mordecai and Esther, the wicked Haman rose up and sought to despoil, and utterly exterminate all Jews, young and old, women and babes, in one day—the thirteenth day of Adar, the twelfth month. But thou, through Thy great mercy, didst frustrate his counsel, and subvert his designs, causing them to recoil on his own head, until he and his sons were hanged on the gallows.'

After the Megillah reading, the following blessing which appears in *Meg.* 21b is chanted: 'Blessed art Thou, God and King of the World, who has contended for us and defended our cause, avenging us by bringing retribution on all our enemies. Blessed art Thou, God and Redeemer, who deliverest Thy people Israel from all their adversaries.'

A eulogy on Mordecai and Esther—*Shoshanat Y'akov* (שׁוֹשַׁנַּת יַעֲקֹב) taken from the Talmud (*Jer. Meg.* iii: 7; *Sopherim* xiv: 6) is then recited. 'The city of Jacob rejoiced and was glad when Mordecai was seen in the purple. Thou hast ever been Israel's salvation, and their hope in every generation, to make known that all who hope in Thee shall not be discomfited, neither shall any be confounded who put their trust in Thee. Accursed by Haman who sought to destroy me; blessed be Mordecai the Jew; accursed by Zeresh, the wife of him that terrifies me. Blessed be Esther my protectress; and may Harbonah also be remembered for good.'

Religious poems (*Kerovot*) (קְרוֹבוֹת) attributed to Kaliri, are inserted in each but one (15th) of the benedictions of the *Amidah*. They recount the Purim story with Midrashic embellishment. *Tahanun* (תַּחֲנוּן) (Supplicatory Prayers) are omitted, as is the *Musaph* (Additional *Amidah*); the latter being added only on New Moons (*Rosh Hodesh*) and *Yomtov* when the Torah ordained additional offerings.

The Talmud originally ordained the *Megillah* reading by day only. To read it at night *only* was not considered as having fulfilled the obligation (*Meg.* 4a). The reading at night may be due to Roman persecutions which prohibited prayer assemblies by Jews during the day. As in many other customs a device intended for a special occasion became the general practice.

Though the Name of God has been deliberately omitted from the Megillah, Purim was regarded by the Jew as 'a divine miracle' (*nes min ha'shamayim*). To quote a non-Jewish commentator on Esther: 'When Esther nerved herself to enter, at the risk of her life, the presence of Ahasuerus, and when she cried out *"How can I endure to see the evil coming upon my people?"* she expressed, without mentioning the name of God, a religious devotion as acceptable to Him as that of Moses or David.'

CHAPTER 4

A PURIM GLOSSARY

Adar

ADAR in an ordinary year has twenty-nine days, in a leap-year thirty. The second Adar has twenty-nine. During the times of the Second Temple, contributions of *Shekalim* were raised at the beginning of this month to pay for the essential services of the Temple. According to the Midrash, Haman chose Adar because of its Zodiac sign *Pisces* (Fish), being heartened in his wicked designs by the words of Jeremiah (xvi: 16): 'Israel will be caught like fish in a net.'

Apart from the traditional dates of the birth and death of Moses on the seventh of Adar, the memorable dates of this month are the *thirteenth* (*Ta'anit Esther*), the *fourteenth* (*Purim*) and the *fifteenth* (*Shushan Purim*). In a leap year, the festival and fast are observed in the *Second* Adar, with the corresponding dates in the first Adar honoured as a minor Purim (*Katan*).

Ta'anit Esther תַּעֲנִית אֶסְתֵּר

Ta'anit Esther is the name given to the fast on the eve of Purim. Its origin is the command Esther gave the Jews of Shushan, through Mordecai, to fast for three days before her uninvited appearance before Ahasuerus (iv: 16). Since a fast of three days' duration would be imposing upon a community a burden greater than it could bear, the Talmudic Rabbis deemed it expedient to reduce it to one day. In the event of the *thirteenth* occurring on a Friday or Saturday, the fast takes place on the Thursday preceding. As this is not the procedure followed in such cases, when the fast is postponed to the Sunday following, a word of explanation is necessary. Alone of the other national fasts of the Jewish year, *Ta'anit Esther* does not proclaim a calamity, but a great act of salvation. In such a case there is no need to postpone 'the evil hour'.

Purim

Purim is a word of Persian origin, quoted in the *Megillah* (iii: 7; ix: 26) to denote the 'lots' cast by Haman by which to determine the most auspicious month and day for the execution of his diabolical plan. Although, together with Hanukkah it is referred to as a 'minor' festival—this is only because work is permitted thereon—Purim is a festival in which is integrated the essential teachings of Judaism, faith, hope and charity. The bitter experience of our people in the *diaspora* has made Purim significant. Various historical sources record almost a hundred such miraculous deliverances which occurred the world over, not necessarily on the traditional date of Purim but identical enough with the main plot to be called Purim. 'In every generation did they arise against us to destroy us; but the Holy One, Blessed be He, constantly delivered us from their hands.'

loah Manot מִשְׁלֹחַ מָנוֹת (Sending of Gifts)

piness was born a twin. To be happy, one must
others happy, especially those less fortunate. The
m of distributing gifts as an essential feature of
m is mentioned in the *Megillah* (ix: 19), and is observed to this day. It is on such customs that the Jewish
reputation for world-wide philanthropy has been fed.
Since the word *manot* (gifts) is in the plural (from the
singular *manah* ('portion'), traditional interpretation
rules that at least *two* gifts be sent. Often they consisted
of special Purim delicacies, such as home-made *Haman-
taschen*, salted almonds, fragrantly-spiced beans, wine,
and grapes. Sums of money were included, should the
recipients be in need.

In this custom, too, the Jewish proverbial love for the
young manifested itself. To inculcate feelings of
generosity in youthful hearts, this assignment of trans-
porting the *mishloah manot* (popularly called *shallah
manot*) was entrusted to them.

The Festive Meal סְעוּדָה (Se'udah)

The banquet occupies a unique and prominent place
in the Book of Esther. It was at a banquet that Vashti,
the beautiful queen of the sottish Ahasuerus was
dismissed from royal favour for refusing to pander to
her consorts' unworthy whims. At a later banquet,
Esther was crowned in her stead; at a banquet also,
Haman received his deserts. His machinations foiled, he
was sentenced to hang on the gallows prepared for

Mordecai. His fate calls to mind the teaching of t͏̴
Mishnah: 'You are measured by the measure w͏̴
which you had intended to measure others.' The sk͏̴
which Hillel addressed, as it floated on the water's
surface, often swims before our horizon as we tramp
life's highways and bye-ways. 'Because thou hast
drowned others, thou wilt be drowned; and those that
drowned thee, will themselves be drowned.'

To eat without words of Torah said at the table was
considered the height of impropriety. So special table-
hymns (*Zemirot*) (זְמִירוֹת) were composed for the
Purim *Se'udah*, as for Shabbat. One famous hymn
began with the alternate refrains 'Blessed be Mordecai,'
and 'Cursed be Haman.' It was once the custom for
strolling players to interrupt the long festive meal with
masquerade and song. As a reward for their labours, and
to the accompaniment of their usual ditty:

> *Today is Purim,*
> *Tomorrow is not;*
> *So give me a coin,*
> *And throw me out*

they were laden with gifts in money or in kind. It was
by such pleasant and innocent means that our ancestors
chased away the shadows of suffering in the *Golah*.

Ad-lo-yada עַד־לֹא־יָדַע

The statement of Rabba (*Meg.* 7b) that 'a man is in
duty bound to be so happy (*li'be'sume*) (לִבְסוּמֵי) on
Purim till he knows not (*ad-lo-yada*) whether to curse
Haman and bless Mordecai, or the reverse,' gave this

new word to modern Hebrew. That the Talmud did not approve of the literal implementation of this hectic advice of Rabba is proved by the story which follows. Two Rabbis, Rabbah and Zeira, indulged to such an excess that Rabbah had, no doubt in fun, injured his colleague and thought him dead. His fervent prayer restored him to life again. The fact that the Talmud concludes this incident with the warning that 'miracles are not a daily occurrence' is evidence of its disapproval of such license.

In the State of Israel, the word *ad-lo-yada* designates not drinking to excess but the spirit of carnival with masquerades, processions, balls, and festivities which are the order of the day, reaching their climax in Tel Aviv. There the streets, re-named for the nonce after the *dramatis personæ* of the Purim plot and through which living *tableaux* of Biblical and modern episodes in our national history are depicted on every conceivable vehicle on wheels. These *ad-lo-yadas* last often until dawn. In the face of such a happy exploitation of a casual Talmudic statement, it would be pedantic to challenge the generally accepted interpretation of Rabba's statement with the argument that what the words really mean is: 'A man must find such cheer in the story of Purim with its lesson over ultimate hope in *divine* salvation, so as not to attach much importance to the parts played either by Mordecai or Haman.'

CHAPTER 5

IN LIGHTER VEIN

Purim Potpourri

THE *Jewish Encyclopedia* (s.v. Purim) lists twenty-nine Purims commemorated in various communities in gratitude for some deliverance. These did not necessarily occur on the Biblical date, but their plot and sequel have identical traits. Leopold Zunz (1794-1886) enumerates *forty* such Purims in his *Zur Geschichte und Literatur* (1845). In the Purim anthology, published in *Sepher Ha'Moadim* (Tel Aviv, 5715), this number has increased to eighty-eight.

We have discussed the possible reasons for the absence of God's name in the Megillah. This omission is rectified in the apocryphal addition called 'The Prayer of Esther,' where the Name appears several times. Equally significant is the omission of the name of Eretz Israel. One would have thought that uppermost in the prayers of our Persian ancestors would have been nostalgic feelings for the Holy Land.

The word *mishteh* (מִשְׁתֶּה) (a feast) occurs *twenty* times in the Megillah; that is, as many times as it occurs in the entire Bible; and the longest sentence in the Torah is *Esther* viii: 19, which comprises forty-three words in the Hebrew original and takes ninety words in English.

Under the Turkish *régime*, Arabs used to refer to Purim as *aid al-sukhar*, 'the festival of sweet things!' In the atmosphere of good will then prevailing Jews sent '*Mishloah Manot*' to Arab friends.

That Purim is popular even among non-Jews is evidenced from the fact that there are cities named after Esther in some States of America. The custom once prevailed in Bombay for many to paint their faces and garments with a red-rose paint on Purim day, and to carry in procession models of their enemies in clay or wood which they formally buried.

It would be true to say that just as the early miracle plays in medieval England occasioned the rise of the drama which, in the skilful hands of a Shakespeare and Decker, or a Beaumont and Fletcher flowered to their maturity, so did Jewish playwrights receive their inspiration first from the Purim story and later from the other incidents graphically portrayed in the Bible. It seems that the first dramatization of Purim began in Italy about 500 years ago, spreading in the course of time to Germany, Russia and Poland. Effigies of Haman and his ten wicked sons, not forgetting his scheming and ambitious wife Zeresh, were suspended from the outer walls of the synagogue, at which children threw missiles.

When the tongue of calumny spread the false rumour that Jews were, in reality, reviling the Christian Saviour under the guise of Haman, a halt was called to this ebullient custom. The theory has been advanced that this sporting with an imaginary foe was primarily responsible for the Blood Libels, in which Jews were accused of slaying a Christian child before Pesah in order to use its blood for baking Matzot.

This custom found no defenders among Jews, though that of greeting Haman's name with noise did. R. Meir Isserles (1525-72) in his glosses to Karo's *Shulhan Arukh* (*Orah Hayim* 690 17) warns: 'It is not right to decide or nullify any custom; for it must have originally served a worthy purpose.'

Purim in Parody

A more dignified form of celebration was devised by Kalonymos b. Kalonymos (1286-1328). Author of *Even Bochan* (The Stone of Examination), he is famous also for his skilful '*Massechet Purim*', a parody to be enjoyed best during the *Se'udah*. In compiling this satire, his aim may have been to wean people away from the vices attending masquerades and indulgence in alcohol which were the order of his day. As happens often, his good intentions were misunderstood by rigid Rabbinic authorities, who could only see in this parody with its subtle use of Talmudic dialectic and style, a blasphemy of the Oral Law. Kalonymos must have been extremely versatile, for he translated into Hebrew a number of Arabic works in mathematics and philosophy. A fascinating chapter in Phillip Goodman's *Purim Anthology* is 'Purim Parody in Jewish literature' (pp. 330-56).

The spirit of parody ignited, it spread like wildfire even into that most unexpected of places—the Yeshivah. There it took most curious shapes. In some places, it was the custom of the *yeshivah bahurim* to rehearse Purim plays to the accompaniment of merry abandon—perhaps the fore-runner of the university 'rag' of today. To this sphere of activity, they attracted roving actors and wandering minstrels. The effect of these 'combined operations' was to lend an artistic touch and festive air to the celebration.

In other *Yeshivot*, there was the custom of electing one of their number as 'Purim Rabbi,' Mock 'Terms of Agreement' were drawn up, in which were stated both his 'duties' and his 'salary.' The *bahur* elected would ape, in guise and gait, speech and mannerism, the august principal, who would often be the one most to enjoy these youthful pranks. It is rumoured that he who first sponsored the institution of the 'Purim Rabbi,' was the founder of the Volozhin Yeshiva—R. Hayim, the favourite pupil of the Gaon of Wilna (1720–97). His intention may have been to provide an annual opportunity for his students, whom he regarded with paternal affection, to criticize any part of the organization they deemed unfair.

Purim has received a new lease of life in the State of Israel. Ghost-like apparitions of festivals and customs have arisen from the sepulchres of ages, have thrown off their shrouds and burst forth clothed in the modern dress of abundant life. The Jewish State has made notable contributions to the stock of parodies and plays associated with the day. One of the most successful theatre shows is the *Purim Play* of J. Silman, produced by Moshe Ha'Levi, the director of the *Ohel* Theatre. The musical scores to this popular Purim entertainment has been written by Emanuel Amiron.

CHAPTER 6

IN DARKER VEIN

PURIM is occasion for merriment. Unfortunately, it is also the origin of virulent antisemitism. This 'dislike of the unlike,' as Israel Zangwill pithily defined it, originated with the accusations made by Haman against Jews. 'And Haman said unto King Ahasuerus: "There is a certain people scattered abroad and dispersed among the peoples in all the provinces of thy kingdom; and their laws are diverse from those of every people; neither keep they the king's laws; therefore it profiteth not the king to suffer them. If it please the king, let it be written that they be destroyed; and I will pay ten thousand talents of silver into the hands of those that have the charge of the king's business, to bring it into the king's treasures."' (*Esther* iii: 8-9.)

This accusation has supplied a text for those who disputed Jewish survival. Improving on Haman, the Alexandrian antisemite Apion (against whose accusations Josephus penned a classic refutation in his *Contra Apionem*) indicts Jews on the following charges: hatred of all other men, clannishness, godlessness, being parasitical, a menace to the Roman Empire. In addition, Jewish bodies emit a peculiar odour, Jews sacrifice a Greek annually for ritual purposes and their claim for superiority is negatived by the fact that they descend from lepers expelled from Egypt. Josephus refuted these assertions, but they are still hurled at Jews; they have been responsible for inquisitions, pogroms, crusades and mass-tortures from the days of Haman to our own.

Racial or Religious Hatred?

Hatred of the Jew may be due to many causes among them being—a dislike of the religious customs to which he unflinchingly clings, or a hatred of the race to which he belongs. The first is best described as anti-Jewish; the second as antisemitic. Both have now merged into the general term antisemitism.

In the age of superstition and religious bigotry, the Jew was hated for his differing faith. '*And their laws are diverse from those of every people.*' With the French Revolution and the dawn of tolerance and liberalism, this hatred moved from religious to racial grounds. Jews were accused of greed, obtrusiveness, lack of social tact and especially of failing in patriotism, echoes of Haman's '*neither keep they the king's laws.*'

Jew-hatred has now almost disappeared, but *antisemitism* has grown into a hydra-headed monster fed by each economic or political crisis, during which the Jew is a convenient scapegoat. Since the Exodus from Egypt, liberty has spoken with a Jewish accent; hence has the Jew been accused of instigating revolutions against tyranny and oppression.

When the hatred of the Jew was based on religious grounds it was possible, in some cases, to seek safety in baptism. Even this escape was barred in Hitler's

Germany, where to possess one Jewish grandparent in four was to qualify for the gas extermination chambers.

Hatred Spur to Re-birth

In all acts of creation pangs must precede birth. The Hebrew language has a phrase for it—חֶבְלֵי לֵדָה *the pangs of birth.'* Similarly, the pangs inflicted upon Jews by their foes, spurred them on to cultural, spiritual and national re-birth. In Russia and Poland it was responsible for the *Haskalah* movement, and the florescence of the *Yeshivot*. The thirty-six years of active Jew-hatred which followed the Russian May laws in 1881 and which culminated in the Bolshevik Revolution of 1917 were creative periods of Russian Jewry. Like Balaam who came to curse, Jewish suffering turned out blessings in disguise. The anti-Jewish measures of Central Europe had their repercussions in France, where the infamous Dreyfus affair occurred in 1894. It was this tragic trial, which moved Herzl to renounce assimilation and turn to the ancient paths which lead to Judaism and nationalism. Three years later the first Zionist Congress was convened in Basle; 51 years later, on Iyar the *fifth*, 5708, the Third Jewish Commonwealth came into being.

'What of the Night?'

We end this chapter on the note on which we began —the accusations of Haman against those whose *'laws are diverse from every other people'*. The comment of the Midrash deserves quotation. Haman said to

81

Ahasuerus: 'Sire, thou wilt do well to persecute the Jews. Their taxes are negligible in amount; they have no government to protect their rights; they are unwilling to serve the king on the pretext that such service interferes with their religious observances. [The exact words of the Midrash are: שה"י ופה"י "It is Shabbat today (שַׁבָּת הַיּוֹם): it is *Pesah* today (פֶּסַח הַיּוֹם)]." They pretend to be busy with their prayers and commemoration of festivals whenever they are called upon to do labour. Moreover, in their prayers they petition God to destroy the evil ones, namely ourselves. They open up their Scroll of the Law and affirm that we are God's enemies.' How modern this sounds!

Here is a later Midrash on the Book of Esther: 'When Esther persuaded Ahasuerus to appoint Mordecai as counsellor, Bigtham and Teresh whom he had superseded in office, said: "Let us kill the king. Everyone will then say: As long as Bigtham and Teresh guarded the king, all was well: no sooner was Mordecai the Jew appointed, than he was murdered. It will then be easy to prove that Jews are not loyal".' By this logic, or better by the lack of it, have those who sought our evil argued their case. There is nothing original in antisemitism.

What is the cure for this malignant spiritual disease, from which the world suffers? Isaiah asked this question: '*Watchman, what of the night? The watchman answereth:* "*The morning has come, so has the night. Enquire diligently into the matter.*"' Torn from their context, these words mean that the darkness of antisemitism will one day be chased away by the light of brotherhood and perfect understanding will prevail between all those whom God has created in His likeness.

The Rabbis discussed the precise moment when night ends and morn floods the sky. This argument was not academic, it being necessary to establish the exact time when the morning *Shema* could be recited. One Rabbi suggested that this moment was when one could discern the blue thread in the fringes from the others which were white. Another said: when one could distinguish the face of a wolf from that of a dog; a third maintained *when one could recognize the face of a brother.*

Only a legal discussion? Yes; but something more. The reproach of antisemitism will be rolled away from the dark, lowering skies of the international scene, when each footsore pilgrim will recognize in all God's children *'the face of a brother.'* The sun of righteousness will then shine, 'with healing in its wings.' The Purim of humanity will then be born.

CHAPTER 7

WINE, JOY AND TEMPERANCE

FEASTING and drinking play a great part in the Purim story. The most important parts of the plot were played at a banquet (מִשְׁתֶּה). It is significant that the Hebrew word for a feast is derived from the verb (שָׁתָה), 'to drink.' In tractate *Megillah*, almost entirely devoted to Purim, we read that 'at the great banquet given by the king, the wine put before each guest hailed from the province whence he came, dating back to the vintage of the year of his birth.' (*ibid*. 12a.) This is a characteristic example of the hyperbole in which the Talmud indulged, but it does express the salient part wine played on that occasion. 'There can be no real joy without meat and wine,' ruled the Talmud. In the Bible, the word *yayin* (wine) occurs no less than 142 times, while cognate words, like שֵׁכָר (old wine), תִּירוֹשׁ (new wine) and חֶמַר (fermented wine), are found twenty-three, thirty-eight and eight times respectively.

This praise of wine was not to encourage drunkenness but merely to point to its potential value if enjoyed in moderation. Just as bread was considered the staple food, so was wine commended as a stimulant for the heavy of heart. (*Prov*. xxxi: 6.) Both together served as signs of good-will and hospitality, as exemplified in the welcome given to Abraham by Malchizedek (Gen.

xiv: 18). Its use, in the metaphorical sense, symbolized
the essence of goodness; the Torah, Israel, Jerusalem,
the Messiah, were compared to wine. The righteous
likened to wine, the wicked were designated as vinegar
— wine turned sour. Hence the bad son of a good father
was styled as (חַלָּא בַּר חַמְרָא) 'vinegar, the son of wine.'
Taken in moderation, it brought health and possessed
prophylactic and curative elements. To economize in
wine was unwise, lest such practice endanger health.
Prudence in its use stimulated the appetite, cheered the
body, satisfied the stomach; such was the prescription of
the doctors of the Talmud. A common blessing in those
far-off days was 'Wine and long life (חַמְרָא וְחַיֵּי) to
the Rabbis and their disciples.' (Shabb. 67b.) It was used
at religious ceremonies, such as Kiddush and Habdalah,
at Grace after Meals and at the meal during which
mourners were comforted. 'It was the greatest of all
medicines; where it is lacking, drugs are necessary.'
(B. Bath. 58b).

Taken immoderately, it brought poverty, suffering,
drunkenness. The remedy for drunkenness was sleep,
so was the advice of the Talmud. 'Wine is strong, but
sleep breaks its force.' (B. Bath. 10a.) Another sage
believed in a long, sharp walk to wear off its effects.
(Erub. 64b.) When taken in excess, man's innermost
secrets will be revealed. But though the Rabbis taught
'Drink not to excess, lest thou sin' (Ber. 29b), Purim
witnessed a general relaxation of these strictures. The
ban was lifted, and the order given that 'a man is in
duty bound to partake of the cup which cheers,' but

here again only when taken in measure. (*Meg.* 7b.) In all things, 'the golden mean' (שְׁבִיל הַזָּהָב) was the counsel of perfection.

A Joyous Faith

Though Sukkot, of all festivals, is designated as 'the season of our rejoicing' (זְמַן שִׂמְחָתֵנוּ), yet every observance of Judaism is impregnated with the joyous spirit. 'Serve ye the Lord with gladness,' is the exhortation of the Psalmist (c: 2). Not least of all Divine commandments is Purim to be commemorated in a merry spirit. The Purim story records: '*The Jews had light and gladness, and joy and honour.*' It will, therefore, not be amiss if we digress for a while to offer a reflection or two on the important place of joy in our faith.

Hebrew possesses more words for joy than any other language. The place it holds in Jewish observance can be gauged from *Deut.* xxviii: 47-48. '*Because thou didst not serve the Lord thy God with joyfulness, and with gladness of heart, by reason of the abundance of all things; therefore shalt thou serve thine enemy whom the Lord shall send against thee, in hunger and in thirst, and in nakedness, and in want of all things; and he shall put a yoke of iron upon thy neck, until he hath destroyed thee.*' The warning is obvious: since you preferred to be miserable when you should have been glad, you will be dejected when you will have proper cause to be so.

Compare the teachings of other ancient faiths with ours to be convinced of its supremacy, a religion which stresses *the joy of duty and the duty of joy.* Psychologists may explain this joyous strain as vital for a people to whom suffering is their badge. More important is it to bear in mind that Jews never allowed persecution to breed bitterness in their souls. Despite torture, we have remained a nation of incurable optimists.

In Judaism, joy is born a twin; to be happy ourselves, we must make others happy. The Midrash on *Deut.* xxvi: 4 says: 'I have hearkened to the voice of the Lord my God, I have done according to all that Thou hast commanded me; that is, I have rejoiced when fulfilling Thy word, and have caused others to rejoice equally.' The story is told in the Talmud (*Ta'anit* 22a) that Elijah once singled out two humble water-carriers in the busy market-place as worthy of eternal life, because their task in life was to cheer the sad. It was the conviction of the Rabbis that God's Presence rests not on laziness, frivolity or sadness, but is a sequel of the joy which is the aftermath of a *Mitzvah* gladly performed.

Though Judaism is a life-long process in self-control it looks askance at a contempt of the good things of life. In the World to Come, says a Rabbi, man will have to give an account for having denied himself of legitimate joys. Even the *Yomim Noraim* (Rosh Ha' shanah and Yom Kippur) must be conspicuous by absence of gloom. '*For this day* (Rosh Ha'shanah) *is holy unto the Lord; neither be ye grieved; for the joy of the Lord is your strength.*' (*Neh.* viii: 10). According to one Rabbi, the joy accompanying the fulfilment of a *Mitzvah* is even more acceptable to God than the actual fulfilment. Another sage makes God say: 'Let a man fulfil my Commandments with joy and it will be considered unto him as righteousness' (*Mechilta* 66b.)

On Purim the joyful intonation of the *Megillah* is a reminder that our liturgy, despite its sombre and austere aspect, is pre-eminently joyous, echoing the *joi-de-vivre* as well as the heart-searchings of the inspired Psalmist. '*But unto all the children of Israel there was light in their habitations.*' (*Ex*. x: 23.) The Jewish home was to be a citadel of joy and peace for the members of the family. To the Jew cheerfulness and hope should be dominant moods, optimism and charity prevailing characteristics and constant communion with God a perennial source of confidence.

Temperance and Moderation

Though a certain relaxation is allowed on Purim yet the Jew, brought up in a strict school of religious discipline, never overstepped the bounds of decency. Despite the festive meal, the mummeries, disguises, doggerels, masques and the election of 'Purim kings' and 'Rabbis'; despite the burning of effigies, the carrying of fir-branches, the whirring of rattles and the blowing of trumpets, the Jew always knew when to draw the line. There was no need for him to sign the 'Pledge' of teetotalism in order to shun drunkenness. His saintly men and women were not celibates. Ecclesiastes (vii: 16-17) advises equi-distance from over-righteousness, as from an excess in wicked practices. This temperance is followed in the reading of the Megillah, where the intonation alternates from the florid and the jubilant when it went well for the Jews, to the despondent and minor key when the Book describes their sad plight, when the influence and ascendency of Haman were at their height. Even the special 'Purim Kiddush,' consisting of a string of irrelevant quotations, was not allowed to minimize the sanctity of the real Kiddush which ushered in the holiness of Shabbat and Yomtov.

The temperance applied in the observance of Purim is due to factors, historical and psychological. The Book of Esther narrates a thrilling deliverance from oppression, emphasizing that behind all human endeavours are the 'Everlasting Arms' which 'move in a mysterious way His manifold wonders to perform.' The rebuke Mordecai gave to Esther (iv: 14) meant: it is the duty of those in high station to help the afflicted, as Moses did when he left a palace to go unto his brethren in bondage. Should they fail in this duty God would help the unfortunate when the time was ripe. This thought introduced solemnity into a festival which might otherwise have become a carnival.

Again: as in the story of Hanukkah, where the foes of the Hasmoneans were not only the soldiers of Antiochus Epiphanes but also the degenerate Hellenists, so also did Haman wax powerful because of the many profligate Persian Jews who took part in the food and drink at the banquets, such participation being contrary to Jewish law.

The psychological factor is also responsible for the moderation of the Jew. Man must strive to present an harmonious integration of the human and the divine; his body coming from earth, his soul from heaven. Coined in 'the image of God,' he possesses the weaknesses to which flesh is heir. To hold the balance between the human and the divine within him were the Biblical commandments given as precision tools with which to chisel out the perfect character. The laws regulating food, hygiene, marital relationship, social life and the whole gamut of Jewish folk-ways have this purpose.

CHAPTER 8

LAST GLEANINGS

PURIM has exerted a tremendous impact on all spheres of Jewish life. Its influence is clearly discernible in Talmud and Midrash, as well as in medieval and modern literature. Especially popular has it been in the work of such famous Yiddish writers as Mendele, Peretz, and Shalom Aleichem, and in the works of Hazaz and Agnon in Israel today. Purim has appealed to poets, from Judah Ha'Levi, Solomon ibn Gabivol, and Immanuel of Rome in medieval times to P. M. Raskin, Judah Cohen, and Nathan Altermann in our own day. In music, drama, folk-song and the arts we find the spirit of Purim. This concluding chapter is in the nature of a postscript in which to emphasize the salient messages of our festival.

The Finger of God   אֶצְבַּע אֱלֹהִים

Though God is not mentioned in the story of Purim He is its inspiration. How else can the choice of Esther be explained, for she lacked, says the Midrash, that feminine charm which turns men's heads. And why was Haman, an important official, so sensitive to the obstinacy of the 'beggar' Mordecai? Who, then, but God caused the pride of Haman to assume such fantastic proportions that his sense of supremacy was disturbed by this solitary act of intransigence?

The more we ponder the real meaning of the story the deeper grows the conviction that the characters in the Megillah were instruments for the Divine purpose. With this in mind the hazardous action of Esther in appearing before the King unbidden, and the invitation extended to him to attend with Haman the private banquet in her apartments become intelligible. We thus possess the code which deciphers the hieroglyphics of the drama. We can now understand why Esther was silent when the King accused Haman of dishonourable intentions towards her (perhaps one of the most eloquent silences in history), when a word of defence on her part might have changed the whole turn of events. It was God who made Ahasuerus assure Esther that any request from her would be fulfilled—'*until half the kingdom, and it shall be given unto thee.*'

To the 'Higher Critics' of the Bible the Book of Esther presents many improbabilities; not so, however, to the eye of faith. As we have seen in the first chapter, nothing conclusive has been advanced to challenge its rightful place in Scripture. Its divinity is seen in the fact that although it records scenes of banqueting, it does not copy Virgil's *Aeniad* in describing its object as '*Arma virumque cano,*' 'I sing of arms and heroism.' The author of the Megillah focuses attention on the unswerving loyalty of Mordecai and Esther, who places her life in jeopardy for the survival of her people.

One of the messages of Purim is that faith in God is more often cradled in the womb of suffering than in the lap of luxury. To quote the Talmud (*Meg.* 14a): 'All the forty-eight Prophets in the Bible could not by their exhortations bring about that which was successfully achieved by the single act of Ahaseurus when he handed the ring of office to Haman with which to seal the fate of the Jews.' The festival assures us that 'God creates the remedy before He inflicts the wound.' (*Meg.* 13b.) It was only after Mordecai had saved the King from the plot against his life, and after Esther had found favour with the King, that God raised Haman as the tool of His vengeance against a people that had grievously sinned.

The nature of this sin is discussed in the Talmud (*Meg.* 12a). Whereas some sages attribute this to the fact that Jews in Susa (Shushan) partook of the forbidden food offered at the royal banquets, others think that it was because their ancestors had bowed the knee to the idol which Nebuchadnezzar had erected in the Temple. The chief point is that salvation came after the Jews had fasted and prayed and re-dedicated themselves to an unswerving obedience of the Torah. 'There is a long way which is short, and a short way which is long,' the great R. Johanan taught. The philosophy of Purim is that Israel will survive not by the destruction of its Hamans, as by the raising of generations of Mordecais and Esthers to whom Judaism will not be a 'misfortune,' as it was to Heine, but the pattern and standard of nobility.

The Secret of Esther

True to the Rabbinic belief that Esther was merely a vehicle for God's salvation, some sages disillusion us completely as to her physical beauty. God chooses the humblest objects as His agents. Moses was chosen as Israel's deliverer from Egypt, though he stammered. It was Sinai, humblest of hill-tops, which was selected as the rostrum from which the Decalogue was proclaimed. The idea may have been to stress that it was not human agency which was responsible for deliverance. Accordingly, Esther was not chosen for her beauty, as for her independence of spirit and her unshakable confidence in the sense of right and wrong. It was the untapped reserves of character which she possessed in abundance that fascinated the King. The fact that she refused the cosmetics liberally offered to the applicants for a consort's crown fascinated the King.

Not all the Rabbis were so unchivalrous. One of them votes her of the four most beautiful women ever created. So fair was she, that her appearance before the monarch eclipsed in radiance all the dusky beauties who had been arrayed in glamorous parade. With Midrashic hyperbole, we are told that when Esther was first ushered into that momentous audience-chamber all were dazzled by her charm, gazing in adoration at that mysterious newcomer from nowhere. All this without the aid of adornments gratuitously offered to make the maidens more pleasing to the royal eye. Although the real reason for the choice of Esther, unguessable in the mists of time, will never be definitely known, there can be little doubt of 'the finger of God' in her selection by Providence for a sublime mission.

Lest We Forget

We observe Purim to recall lessons we cannot afford to forget. Chief among them is that the Jew can never substitute trust in human power for unshakable faith in God. The Midrash tells us that the majority of Jews in Persia regarded themselves as Persians first, Jews afterwards. These also were not excluded from the general plan of extermination. When our ancestors were exiled from England, France and Spain in 1290, 1392 and 1492 C.E. respectively, there went with them those whose attachment to Judaism was of the frailest kind. A similar tale can be told of the victims of Nazi bestiality in our own days. At least, those who have God in their hearts carry this faith to sustain them in their exile with hope to await the appearance of the rainbow after the flood. Those of little faith have not even this.

Purim proclaims a stern reminder for our foes; they will be caught in the trap they had planned for others. Little did Haman realize when he set up 'the gallows of fifty cubits high' that he and his ten ungallant sons would one day dangle from them. History has always shown that the eternal Jewish people stands at the grave of its persecutors, 'exhausting Time and encroaching upon Eternity.'

As we listen to the intonation of the Megillah, enriched by various melodic shades, skilfully combining mournful, martial and joyous *motifs*, reflecting the tears, fasting and grief, as well as the fluctuating fortunes, triumphs and joys—all so adroitly woven into the traditional chanting—we become conscious of our frailty when pitted against the omnipotence of God.